This diary belongs to

....

First published in 2025
by Faber & Faber Ltd
The Bindery
51 Hatton Garden
London EC1N 8HN

Designed and typeset by Faber & Faber Ltd
Printed in Turkey

All rights reserved
Poems © contributors' own

This book is covered in Liberty Fabrics' Archive Gingham
Copyright © Liberty Fabrics Limited 2025

Clauses in the Banking and Financial Dealings Act allow the government to alter dates at short notice

A CIP record for this book is available from the British Library

ISBN 978−0−571−39570−5

Our authorised representative in the EU for product safety is
Easy Access System Europe, Mustamäe tee 50, 10621 Tallinn, Estonia
gpsr.requests@easproject.com

Faber & Faber was founded in 1929 ...

... but its roots go back further to the Scientific Press, which started publishing in the early years of the century. The press's largest shareholders were Sir Maurice and Lady Gwyer, and their desire to expand into general publishing led them to Geoffrey Faber, a fellow of All Souls College, Oxford. Faber and Gwyer was founded in 1925. After four years Faber took the company forward alone, and the story goes that Walter de la Mare suggested adding a second, fictitious Faber to balance the company name.

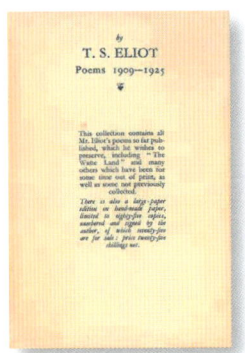

In the meantime, the firm had prospered. T. S. Eliot, who had been suggested to Geoffrey Faber by a colleague at All Souls, had left Lloyds Bank in London to join him as a director, and in its first season the firm issued Eliot's *Poems 1909–1925*. In addition, the catalogues from the early years included books by Jean Cocteau, Herbert Read and Vita Sackville-West.

Poetry was always to be a significant element in the list and under Eliot's aegis Marianne Moore, Louis MacNeice and David Jones soon joined Ezra Pound, W. H. Auden, Stephen Spender, James Joyce, Siegfried Sassoon, D. H. Lawrence and Walter de la Mare.

Under Geoffrey Faber's chairmanship the board in 1929 included Eliot, Richard de la Mare, Charles Stewart and Frank Morley. This young team built up a comprehensive and profitable catalogue distinguished by modern design, much of which is still in print. Biographies, memoirs, fiction, poetry, political and religious essays, art and architecture monographs, children's books and a pioneering range of ecology titles contributed towards an eclectic list full of character. Faber also produced Eliot's groundbreaking literary review *The Criterion*.

The Second World War brought both paper shortages and higher taxes, and the post-war years continued to be difficult. However, as the economy recovered a new generation of poets joined Faber, including Robert Lowell, Ted Hughes, Sylvia Plath, Seamus Heaney, Philip Larkin and Thom Gunn.

Each decade that followed would see the addition of exciting new poets who were among the finest of their generation.

In over ninety years of publishing, Faber has been the home of Nobel Prize-winning poets Derek Walcott (1992), Seamus Heaney (1995) and Wisława Szymborska (1996); the poet laureates Ted Hughes (appointed 1984) and Andrew Motion (appointed 1999); and the current poet laureate, Simon Armitage (appointed 2019).

The year 2026 finds the company that Geoffrey Faber founded remaining true to the principles he instigated and independent of corporate ownership. The Faber poetry list continues to flourish, as evinced by the talent on display in the pages of this diary.

A more detailed chronology of Faber & Faber's poetry publishing appears at the back of this diary.

Death of a Naturalist

by Seamus Heaney

ANNUAL CALENDARS 2026

JANUARY
M	T	W	T	F	S	S
29	30	31	1	2	3	4
5	6	7	8	9	10	11
12	13	14	15	16	17	18
19	20	21	22	23	24	25
26	27	28	29	30	31	1
2	3	4	5	6	7	8

FEBRUARY
M	T	W	T	F	S	S
26	27	28	29	30	31	1
2	3	4	5	6	7	8
9	10	11	12	13	14	15
16	17	18	19	20	21	22
23	24	25	26	27	28	1
2	3	4	5	6	7	8

MARCH
M	T	W	T	F	S	S
23	24	25	26	27	28	1
2	3	4	5	6	7	8
9	10	11	12	13	14	15
16	17	18	19	20	21	22
23	24	25	26	27	28	29
30	31	1	2	3	4	5

APRIL
M	T	W	T	F	S	S
30	31	1	2	3	4	5
6	7	8	9	10	11	12
13	14	15	16	17	18	19
20	21	22	23	24	25	26
27	28	29	30	1	2	3
4	5	6	7	8	9	10

MAY
M	T	W	T	F	S	S
27	28	29	30	1	2	3
4	5	6	7	8	9	10
11	12	13	14	15	16	17
18	19	20	21	22	23	24
25	26	27	28	29	30	31
1	2	3	4	5	6	7

JUNE
M	T	W	T	F	S	S
1	2	3	4	5	6	7
8	9	10	11	12	13	14
15	16	17	18	19	20	21
22	23	24	25	26	27	28
29	30	1	2	3	4	5
6	7	8	9	10	11	12

JULY
M	T	W	T	F	S	S
29	30	1	2	3	4	5
6	7	8	9	10	11	12
13	14	15	16	17	18	19
20	21	22	23	24	25	26
27	28	29	30	31	1	2
3	4	5	6	7	8	9

AUGUST
M	T	W	T	F	S	S
27	28	29	30	31	1	2
3	4	5	6	7	8	9
10	11	12	13	14	15	16
17	18	19	20	21	22	23
24	25	26	27	28	29	30
31	1	2	3	4	5	6

SEPTEMBER
M	T	W	T	F	S	S
31	1	2	3	4	5	6
7	8	9	10	11	12	13
14	15	16	17	18	19	20
21	22	23	24	25	26	27
28	29	30	1	2	3	4
5	6	7	8	9	10	11

OCTOBER
M	T	W	T	F	S	S
28	29	30	1	2	3	4
5	6	7	8	9	10	11
12	13	14	15	16	17	18
19	20	21	22	23	24	25
26	27	28	29	30	31	1
2	3	4	5	6	7	8

NOVEMBER
M	T	W	T	F	S	S
26	27	28	29	30	31	1
2	3	4	5	6	7	8
9	10	11	12	13	14	15
16	17	18	19	20	21	22
23	24	25	26	27	28	29
30	1	2	3	4	5	6

DECEMBER
M	T	W	T	F	S	S
30	1	2	3	4	5	6
7	8	9	10	11	12	13
14	15	16	17	18	19	20
21	22	23	24	25	26	27
28	29	30	31	1	2	3
4	5	6	7	8	9	10

2025

JANUARY
M	T	W	T	F	S	S
30	31	1	2	3	4	5
6	7	8	9	10	11	12
13	14	15	16	17	18	19
20	21	22	23	24	25	26
27	28	29	30	31	1	2
3	4	5	6	7	8	9

FEBRUARY
M	T	W	T	F	S	S
27	28	29	30	31	1	2
3	4	5	6	7	8	9
10	11	12	13	14	15	16
17	18	19	20	21	22	23
24	25	26	27	28	1	2
3	4	5	6	7	8	9

MARCH
M	T	W	T	F	S	S
24	25	26	27	28	1	2
3	4	5	6	7	8	9
10	11	12	13	14	15	16
17	18	19	20	21	22	23
24	25	26	27	28	29	30
31	1	2	3	4	5	6

APRIL
M	T	W	T	F	S	S
31	1	2	3	4	5	6
7	8	9	10	11	12	13
14	15	16	17	18	19	20
21	22	23	24	25	26	27
28	29	30	1	2	3	4
5	6	7	8	9	10	11

MAY
M	T	W	T	F	S	S
28	29	30	1	2	3	4
5	6	7	8	9	10	11
12	13	14	15	16	17	18
19	20	21	22	23	24	25
26	27	28	29	30	31	1
2	3	4	5	6	7	8

JUNE
M	T	W	T	F	S	S
26	27	28	29	30	31	1
2	3	4	5	6	7	8
9	10	11	12	13	14	15
16	17	18	19	20	21	22
23	24	25	26	27	28	29
30	1	2	3	4	5	6

JULY
M	T	W	T	F	S	S
30	1	2	3	4	5	6
7	8	9	10	11	12	13
14	15	16	17	18	19	20
21	22	23	24	25	26	27
28	29	30	31	1	2	3
4	5	6	7	8	9	10

AUGUST
M	T	W	T	F	S	S
28	29	30	31	1	2	3
4	5	6	7	8	9	10
11	12	13	14	15	16	17
18	19	20	21	22	23	24
25	26	27	28	29	30	31
1	2	3	4	5	6	7

SEPTEMBER
M	T	W	T	F	S	S
1	2	3	4	5	6	7
8	9	10	11	12	13	14
15	16	17	18	19	20	21
22	23	24	25	26	27	28
29	30	1	2	3	4	5
6	7	8	9	10	11	12

OCTOBER
M	T	W	T	F	S	S
29	30	1	2	3	4	5
6	7	8	9	10	11	12
13	14	15	16	17	18	19
20	21	22	23	24	25	26
27	28	29	30	31	1	2
3	4	5	6	7	8	9

NOVEMBER
M	T	W	T	F	S	S
27	28	29	30	31	1	2
3	4	5	6	7	8	9
10	11	12	13	14	15	16
17	18	19	20	21	22	23
24	25	26	27	28	29	30
1	2	3	4	5	6	7

DECEMBER
M	T	W	T	F	S	S
1	2	3	4	5	6	7
8	9	10	11	12	13	14
15	16	17	18	19	20	21
22	23	24	25	26	27	28
29	30	31	1	2	3	4
5	6	7	8	9	10	11

2027

JANUARY
M	T	W	T	F	S	S
28	29	30	31	1	2	3
4	5	6	7	8	9	10
11	12	13	14	15	16	17
18	19	20	21	22	23	24
25	26	27	28	29	30	31
1	2	3	4	5	6	7

FEBRUARY
M	T	W	T	F	S	S
1	2	3	4	5	6	7
8	9	10	11	12	13	14
15	16	17	18	19	20	21
22	23	24	25	26	27	28
1	2	3	4	5	6	7
8	9	10	11	12	13	14

MARCH
M	T	W	T	F	S	S
1	2	3	4	5	6	7
8	9	10	11	12	13	14
15	16	17	18	19	20	21
22	23	24	25	26	27	28
29	30	31	1	2	3	4
5	6	7	8	9	10	11

APRIL
M	T	W	T	F	S	S
29	30	31	1	2	3	4
5	6	7	8	9	10	11
12	13	14	15	16	17	18
19	20	21	22	23	24	25
26	27	28	29	30	1	2
3	4	5	6	7	8	9

MAY
M	T	W	T	F	S	S
26	27	28	29	30	1	2
3	4	5	6	7	8	9
10	11	12	13	14	15	16
17	18	19	20	21	22	23
24	25	26	27	28	29	30
31	1	2	3	4	5	6

JUNE
M	T	W	T	F	S	S
31	1	2	3	4	5	6
7	8	9	10	11	12	13
14	15	16	17	18	19	20
21	22	23	24	25	26	27
28	29	30	1	2	3	4
5	6	7	8	9	10	11

JULY
M	T	W	T	F	S	S
28	29	30	1	2	3	4
5	6	7	8	9	10	11
12	13	14	15	16	17	18
19	20	21	22	23	24	25
26	27	28	29	30	31	1
2	3	4	5	6	7	8

AUGUST
M	T	W	T	F	S	S
26	27	28	29	30	31	1
2	3	4	5	6	7	8
9	10	11	12	13	14	15
16	17	18	19	20	21	22
23	24	25	26	27	28	29
30	31	1	2	3	4	5

SEPTEMBER
M	T	W	T	F	S	S
30	31	1	2	3	4	5
6	7	8	9	10	11	12
13	14	15	16	17	18	19
20	21	22	23	24	25	26
27	28	29	30	1	2	3
4	5	6	7	8	9	10

OCTOBER
M	T	W	T	F	S	S
27	28	29	30	1	2	3
4	5	6	7	8	9	10
11	12	13	14	15	16	17
18	19	20	21	22	23	24
25	26	27	28	29	30	31
1	2	3	4	5	6	7

NOVEMBER
M	T	W	T	F	S	S
1	2	3	4	5	6	7
8	9	10	11	12	13	14
15	16	17	18	19	20	21
22	23	24	25	26	27	28
29	30	1	2	3	4	5
6	7	8	9	10	11	12

DECEMBER
M	T	W	T	F	S	S
29	30	1	2	3	4	5
6	7	8	9	10	11	12
13	14	15	16	17	18	19
20	21	22	23	24	25	26
27	28	29	30	31	1	2
3	4	5	6	7	8	9

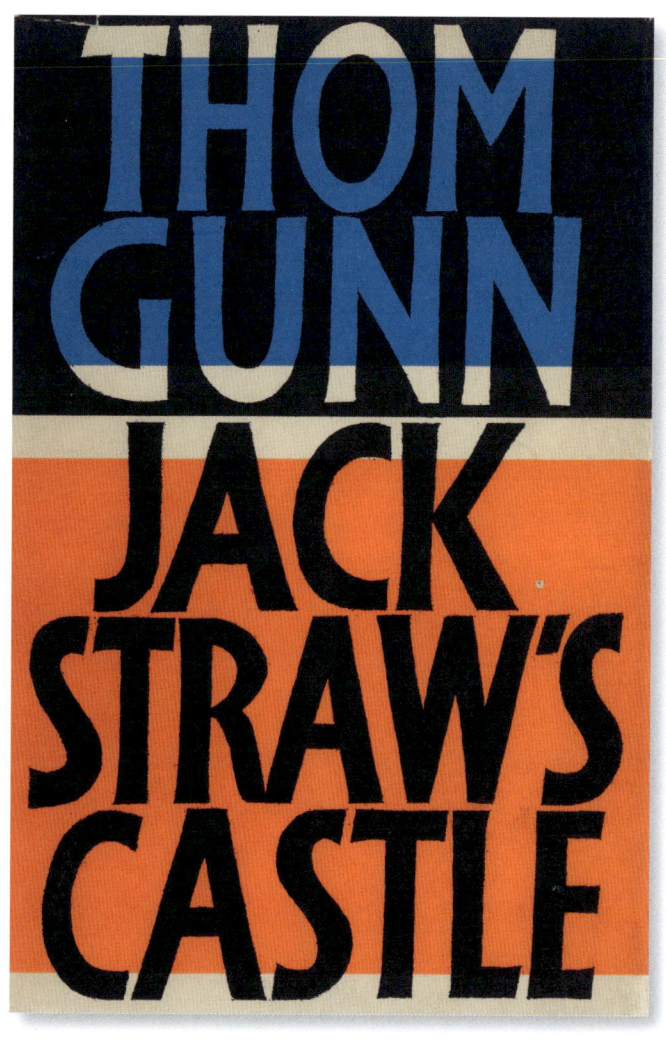

DECEMBER 2025 / JANUARY 2026

29 Monday

30 Tuesday

31 Wednesday NEW YEAR'S EVE

1 Thursday NEW YEAR'S DAY

2 Friday 2ND JANUARY HOLIDAY (SCT)
DAY AFTER NEW YEAR'S DAY (NZ)

3 Saturday

4 Sunday

WILLIAM BLAKE

A Divine Image

Cruelty has a Human Heart,
And Jealousy a Human Face;
Terror the Human Form Divine,
And Secrecy the Human Dress.

The Human Dress is forged Iron,
The Human Form a fiery Forge,
The Human Face a Furnace seal'd,
The Human Heart its hungry Gorge.

POET TO POET *William Blake: Poems Selected by James Fenton* (2010)

JANUARY 2026

5 Monday

6 Tuesday

7 Wednesday

8 Thursday

9 Friday

10 Saturday   11 Sunday

MATTHEW FRANCIS

Wind

after Dafydd ap Gwilym

Who sent you, messenger, running without any feet,
all puff and scurry but never out of breath?
First you're all over me, then you're off
over the next hill before
I've laid eyes on you.

Don't waste your sighs on me. There's a song in you somewhere
among all those leaves and seeds, the pocket-fluff
you carry in the folds of yourself.
Sing it around her house where
my voice can't reach her.

Trespasser traipsing through cornfields, no one can stop you.
Berserker havocking among oak branches,
you play in the surf, whippersnapper,
a restless host to the rain
that nests in your hair.

The Green Month (2025)

JANUARY 2026

12 Monday

13 Tuesday

14 Wednesday

15 Thursday

16 Friday

17 Saturday		18 Sunday

DALJIT NAGRA

from Ramayana

The Supreme Being alone is timeless
and suffers neither birth nor death nor growth.
Such a one is void of beginning or end.
           Or in-between.

Such a one is only you, Rama.
Rama, you are Vishnu
   but you are more than Vishnu.
If you are not, Rama, existence is mere air.

You are the mantra, the syllable sacred.
   The unknown, the unknowable
even to yourself.

In yourself you are a billion eyes and a billion feet
   and you uphold time
     by living in all that lives.

You are everything that dies and everything that revives.
You are the element, the space and the depth entire.
You are the range. The range unbound.

          Rama, you are God.

Sita is purer than light. Sita is Lakshmi.
Sita is the journey of your existence,
   the plenitude of your source.
Rama, without Sita you are mere air.

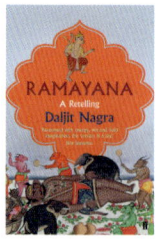

Ramayana (2013)

JANUARY 2026

19 Monday

20 Tuesday

21 Wednesday

22 Thursday

23 Friday

24 Saturday

25 Sunday   BURNS NIGHT

MARY JEAN CHAN

from Ars Poetica XI

This is the myth of love's tenderness:
that it only heals and cannot wound.
After thirty years of spinning around
in space, you hear echoes, wilderness
among stars devoid of human tempers.
Linger there – it is quiet – your breath
audible as the staccato burn on a hearth.
Dear reader, how often are you tempted
to infidelity with words: those curious
shapes that simply demand you listen?
Offer a translation your life can bear.
Revisit poems that spark mysterious
doorways in the mind and glistening
eyes. Let ink seep into what you hear.

Bright Fear (2023)

JANUARY / FEBRUARY 2026

26 Monday AUSTRALIA DAY (AUS)

27 Tuesday

28 Wednesday

29 Thursday

30 Friday

31 Saturday   1 Sunday

Paul Muldoon
Joy in Service on Rue Tagore

Poetry

ff

FEBRUARY 2026

2 Monday ST BRIGID'S DAY (IRL)

3 Tuesday

4 Wednesday

5 Thursday

6 Friday WAITANGI DAY (NZ)

7 Saturday

8 Sunday

SEAMUS HEANEY

Miracle

Not the one who takes up his bed and walks
But the ones who have known him all along
And carry him in —

Their shoulders numb, the ache and stoop deeplocked
In their backs, the stretcher handles
Slippery with sweat. And no let-up

Until he's strapped on tight, made tiltable
And raised to the tiled roof, then lowered for healing.
Be mindful of them as they stand and wait

For the burn of the paid-out ropes to cool,
Their slight lightheadedness and incredulity
To pass, those ones who had known him all along.

100 Poems (2018)

FEBRUARY 2026

9 Monday

10 Tuesday

11 Wednesday

12 Thursday

13 Friday

14 Saturday   VALENTINE'S DAY   15 Sunday

D. H. LAWRENCE

Sea-Weed

Sea-weed sways and sways and swirls
as if swaying were its form of stillness;
and if it flushes against fierce rock
it slips over it as shadows do, without hurting itself.

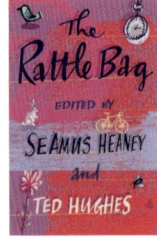

The Rattle Bag (2005)

FEBRUARY 2026

16 Monday

17 Tuesday

18 Wednesday

19 Thursday

20 Friday

21 Saturday

22 Sunday

GILLIAN CLARKE

Cadfannan

Caeog, cynifiad, cywlad rwyd,
Rhuthr eryr yn ebyr pan llithiwyd.
Ei amod a fu nod a gadwyd,
Gwell gwnaeth ei arfaeth, ni giliwyd.
Rhag byddin Ododdin odechwyd,
Hydr gymell ar freithell Fanawyd,
Ni noddi nac ysgedd nac ysgwyd.
Ni ellid, onid ryfaethpwyd,
Rhag ergyd Cadfannan cadwyd.

*

Flaunting a brooch, snare of the enemy,
fish-eagle of the estuary,

purposeful, steady,
a promise kept.

The land of Manawyd within sight,
Gododdin put the foe to flight,

Armour and shield could not save them.
None but the nourished fought Cadfannan.

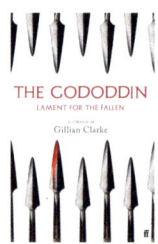

The Gododdin (2021)

FEBRUARY / MARCH 2026

23 Monday

24 Tuesday

25 Wednesday

26 Thursday

27 Friday

28 Saturday

1 Sunday ST DAVID'S DAY

An Unexpected Meeting

We treat each other with exceeding courtesy;
we say, it's great to see you after all these years.

Our tigers drink milk.
Our hawks tread the ground.
Our sharks have all drowned.
Our wolves yawn beyond the open cage.

Our snakes have shed their lightning,
our apes their flights of fancy,
our peacocks have renounced their plumes.
The bats flew out of our hair long ago.

We fall silent in midsentence,
all smiles, past help.
Our humans
don't know how to talk to one another.

Poems New and Collected 1957–1997 (1999)

MARCH 2026

2 Monday

3 Tuesday

4 Wednesday

5 Thursday

6 Friday

7 Saturday

8 Sunday

MARCH 2026

9 Monday

10 Tuesday

11 Wednesday

12 Thursday

13 Friday

14 Saturday   15 Sunday

LACHLAN MACKINNON

True Happy Stories

My father played for Harlequins once.

In summer the great rugger players
put out a cricket team and, their slow bowler stuck
on a delayed train, my father was deputed
from the home, the schoolmasters', side.

Their whites gleam
with Corinthian spirit
long, long ago.

Dr Grace, waking early, fished his hosts'
ornamental fountain
of all its goldfish.

Things happen as they should
long, long ago
in the endless imagined summers
that never were,

until they'd vanished, deathless.

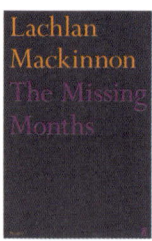

The Missing Months (2022)

MARCH 2026

16 Monday

17 Tuesday ST PATRICK'S DAY (NI, IRL)

18 Wednesday

19 Thursday

20 Friday

21 Saturday HUMAN RIGHTS DAY (ZA)
WORLD POETRY DAY

22 Sunday

ANGE MLINKO

To My Guitarist

Did you ever think, when you cooed
over the delicate snails after rain,
or fed a lettuce leaf to your tortoise,
that your affinity for shelled creatures
revealed one of your own features,
a fear of being soft-bodied, porous,
lacking calcium carbonate or keratin
to house your defenseless solitude?

Those of us with hides like pachyderms
may find it harder to understand.
Remember how, at the turtle hospital,
you sobbed over old uses for tortoiseshell?
I feel it when I take your fretting hand:
the tenderness each callused tip affirms.

Foxglovewise (2025)

MARCH 2026

23 Monday

24 Tuesday

25 Wednesday

26 Thursday

27 Friday

28 Saturday 29 Sunday

EDWARD THOMAS

Thaw

Over the land freckled with snow half-thawed
The speculating rooks at their nests cawed
And saw from elm-tops, delicate as flower of grass,
What we below could not see, Winter pass.

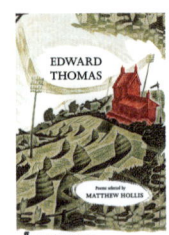

POET TO POET *Edward Thomas: Poems Selected by Matthew Hollis* (2016)

MARCH / APRIL 2026

30 Monday

31 Tuesday

1 Wednesday

2 Thursday

3 Friday   GOOD FRIDAY (UK, AUS, ZA, NZ)

4 Saturday   EASTER (HOLY) SATURDAY

5 Sunday   EASTER SUNDAY

DEREK WALCOTT

The Dormitory

Time is the guide that brings all to a crux,
Who hangs his map will move
Out of the mere geology of books,
To see his valley's palm wrinkled with loves.

These sleep like islands, and I watch sleep lick
Their arms' flung promontories, remove
With individual erasure all their love
Of muscle. Now towards the sea there, I look

Where rippling signatures of water break
Over the sighing dormitories of
The drowned whom soft winds move,
Here these inquiet mouths like rivers speak.

Or from these boys, who in the uncertain luck
Of sleep, expect to live,
The breath curls from their separated lips like
Mists of time that over valleys grieve.

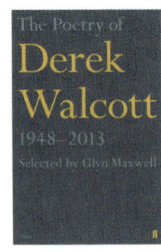

The Poetry of Derek Walcott 1948–2013 (2014)

APRIL 2026

6 Monday   EASTER MONDAY (UK, IRL, AUS, NZ)
                  FAMILY DAY (ZA)

7 Tuesday

8 Wednesday

9 Thursday

10 Friday

11 Saturday   12 Sunday

WENDY COPE

APRIL 2026

13 Monday

14 Tuesday

15 Wednesday

16 Thursday

17 Friday

18 Saturday	19 Sunday

STEPHEN CRANE

'In the desert'

In the desert
I saw a creature, naked, bestial,
Who, squatting upon the ground,
Held his heart in his hands,
And ate of it.
I said, 'Is it good, friend?'
'It is bitter – bitter,' he answered;
'But I like it
Because it is bitter,
And because it is my heart.'

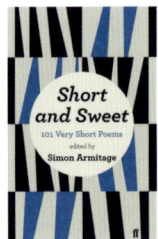

Short and Sweet (2002)

APRIL 2026

20 Monday

21 Tuesday

22 Wednesday

23 Thursday ST GEORGE'S DAY

24 Friday

25 Saturday ANZAC DAY (AUS, NZ)   26 Sunday

dear little b,

I love to see you sat there
pregnant with promise
& nobody's business:

be bodacious if you feel like it.
be camouflaged, if not.

some might say you should be louder, bolder, tall.
uppercase & camera-ready. but little b, you're weary,

aren't you, of being counted in the wrong kinds of ways.
besides, haven't you been capital forever? haven't you

been asterisked for far too long? *no longer,
or not since, or not enough*, some might think

& let them think it, but as for me, little b
I'll be blunt now:

I like the way you lay low
the way you stay low
& keep shooting.

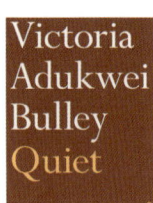

Quiet (2022)

APRIL / MAY 2026

27 **Monday** ANZAC DAY HOLIDAY (AUS, NZ)
FREEDOM DAY (ZA)

28 **Tuesday**

29 **Wednesday**

30 **Thursday**

1 **Friday** WORKERS' DAY (ZA)

2 **Saturday**   3 **Sunday**

BEN JONSON

Witches' Chasm

The owl is abroad, the bat and the toad,
   And so is the cat-a-mountain;
The ant and the mole both sit in a hole,
   And frog peeps out o' the fountain.
The dogs they do bay, and the timbrels play,
   The spindle is now a-turning;
The moon it is red, and the stars are fled,
   But all the sky is a-burning:
The ditch is made, and our nails the spade:
With pictures full, of wax and wool,
Their livers I stick with needles quick;
There lacks but the blood to make up the flood.
Quickly, dame, then bring your part in!
Spur, spur, upon little Martin!
Merrily, merrily, make him sail,
A worm in his mouth and a thorn in's tail,
Fire above, and fire below,
With a whip i' your hand to make him go!

The Rattle Bag (2005)

MAY 2026

4 Monday   EARLY MAY BANK HOLIDAY (UK)
           MAY DAY (IRL)

5 Tuesday

6 Wednesday

7 Thursday

8 Friday

9 Saturday   10 Sunday

RICHARD SCOTT

Red Jasper

Thirty-eight and I am learning a lot about rocks — this stone nurtures, this stone guides, this stone clears, this stone detoxifies.

Red jasper — routinely water-worn, etched, red-shock when split — carries past words, images within its brecciated fissures. Blooded elixir. Is boy-like.

All my life I have been meeting others who suffered the same pressure — sub-atomic, neurological — of a love which is not love at all but instead is this attrition. Red sand.

You shouldn't even think about all that any more says so many people and websites. So I get busy writing poems. Conduits. Shamanic journeys into the sub-mantle realm. It turns out that I am raw, powerful.

I feel my purpose crystallise within me. Scabs — little platelets of red jasper are crusping up, forming over my entire body. Something important is happening to me.

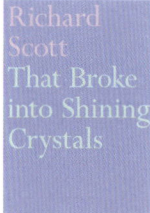

That Broke into Shining Crystals (2025)

MAY 2026

11 Monday

12 Tuesday

13 Wednesday

14 Thursday

15 Friday

16 Saturday				17 Sunday

TOM PAULIN

Tom Paulin
A State of Justice

MAY 2026

18 Monday

19 Tuesday

20 Wednesday

21 Thursday

22 Friday

23 Saturday

24 Sunday

Preludes

IV

His soul stretched tight across the skies
That fade behind a city block,
Or trampled by insistent feet
At four and five and six o'clock;
And short square fingers stuffing pipes,
And evening newspapers, and eyes
Assured of certain certainties,
The conscience of a blackened street
Impatient to assume the world.

I am moved by fancies that are curled
Around these images, and cling:
The notion of some infinitely gentle
Infinitely suffering thing.

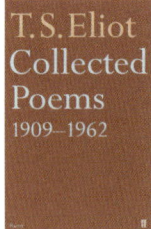

Collected Poems 1909–1962 (2002)

MAY 2026

25 Monday SPRING BANK HOLIDAY (UK)

26 Tuesday

27 Wednesday

28 Thursday

29 Friday

30 Saturday   31 Sunday

Mozart in the Shopping Centre

Three scruffy teenagers
Are playing Mozart in the Brooks
So beautifully that shoppers turn their backs
On Argos, MVC and Waterstones
To stand and listen as the strings
Sing out pure happiness.

There's quite a crowd of us.
I may not be the only one
To blink back tears. It isn't just the music
But the people, sharing this,
Who came out shopping on a rainy Saturday
And chanced on the sublime.

Collected Poems (2024)

JUNE 2026

1 Monday   JUNE BANK HOLIDAY (IRL)
          KING'S BIRTHDAY HOLIDAY (NZ)

2 Tuesday

3 Wednesday

4 Thursday

5 Friday

6 Saturday   7 Sunday

CAMILLE RALPHS

after George Herbert

Come, my Motorway, my Equals Sign, my Higher Race,
such a Motorway as wheels with stars,
such an Equals Sign as time plus space,
such a Higher Race as cable cars.

Come, my Bedside Light, my Takeaway, my Calloused Hand,
such a Bedside Light as lanternfish,
such a Takeaway as takes a stand,
such a Calloused Hand as makes a wish.

Come, my Costume Play, my I Will Yes, my Organ Note,
such a Costume Play as none can dress,
such an I Will Yes as none can quote,
such an Organ Note as plays in yes.

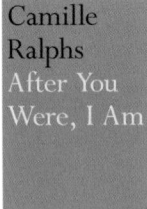

After You Were, I Am (2024)

June 2026

8 Monday

9 Tuesday

10 Wednesday

11 Thursday

12 Friday

13 Saturday

14 Sunday

EMILY BERRY

Song

after Luna Miguel

When I became mermaid it was for this reason.
The girl I love is a beautiful boy.
So you would not ask questions.
Because I gave myself up to the rain
but it was too late; the rain could not save me.
And when I thought the line was straight,
I was wrong; I could not follow the line.
Thus the shore, infinitely. Thus these rocks.
There was so much to feel good and sorry about.
And I shut my legs up tight, I shut my eyes.
So I could see him better, so I could see her.

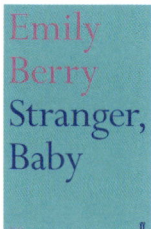

Stranger, Baby (2017)

JUNE 2026

15 Monday

16 Tuesday   YOUTH DAY (ZA)

17 Wednesday

18 Thursday

19 Friday

20 Saturday   21 Sunday

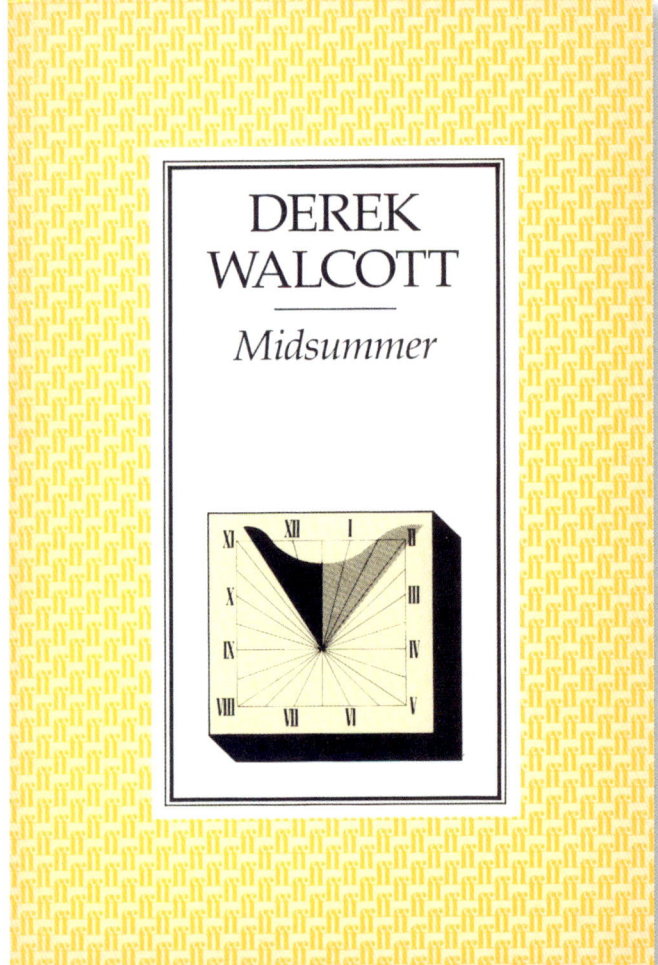

JUNE 2026

22 Monday

23 Tuesday

24 Wednesday

25 Thursday

26 Friday

27 Saturday   28 Sunday

JOHN CLARE

In Hilly Wood

How sweet to be thus nestling deep in boughs
Upon an ashen stoven pillowing me;
Faintly are heard the ploughmen at their ploughs,
But not an eye can find its way to see.
The sunbeams scarce molest me with a smile,
So thick the leafy armies gather round;
And where they do, the breeze blows cool the while,
Their leafy shadows dancing on the ground.
Full many a flower, too, wishing to be seen,
Perks up its head the hiding grass between –
In mid-wood silence, thus, how sweet to be,
Where all the noises that on peace intrude
Come from the chittering cricket, bird and bee,
Whose songs have charms to sweeten solitude.

POET TO POET *John Clare: Poems Selected by Paul Farley* (2011)

JUNE / JULY 2026

29 Monday

30 Tuesday

1 Wednesday

2 Thursday

3 Friday

4 Saturday   5 Sunday

L

This time two weeks before his 13th birthday the Antichrist Pope John Paul II visited his island. With a stub of coal Godspeed drafted new statutes for the Court of Star Chamber on the plyboard side of the school's latrine. He stepped back to admire his new minted theology. 'These are no competent judges of the doctrine of God in Christ but must be overthrown' it declared. It also declared: 'Vatican don't instruct I I instruct Vatican.'

The strength of the battalion stood at 603 officers and 7130 other ranks.

School of Instructions (2023)

JULY 2026

6 Monday

7 Tuesday

8 Wednesday

9 Thursday

10 Friday MATARIKI (NZ)

11 Saturday

12 Sunday BATTLE OF THE BOYNE

JOHN DONNE

from Holy Sonnets

X

Death be not proud, though some have called thee
Mighty and dreadfull, for, thou art not soe,
For, those, whom thou think'st, thou dost overthrow,
Die not, poore death, nor yet canst thou kill mee.
From rest and sleepe, which but thy pictures bee,
Much pleasure, then from thee, much more must flow,
And soonest our best men with thee doe goe,
Rest of their bones, and soules deliverie.
Thou art slave to Fate, Chance, kings, and desperate men,
And dost with poyson, warre, and sicknesse dwell,
And poppie, or charmes can make us sleepe as well,
And better then thy stroake; why swell'st thou then?
One short sleepe past, wee wake eternally,
And death shall be no more; death, thou shalt die.

POET TO POET *John Donne: Poems Selected by Paul Muldoon* (2012)

JULY 2026

13 Monday   BATTLE OF THE BOYNE HOLIDAY (NI)

14 Tuesday

15 Wednesday

16 Thursday

17 Friday

18 Saturday   19 Sunday

WILLIAM SHAKESPEARE

Sonnet 49

Against that time, if ever that time come,
When I shall see thee frown on my defects;
When as thy love hath cast his utmost sum,
Called to that audit by advised respects;
Against that time when thou shalt strangely pass,
And scarcely greet me with that sun, thine eye;
When love, converted from the thing it was,
Shall reasons find of settled gravity;
Against that time do I ensconce me here,
Within the knowledge of mine own desert,
And this my hand, against my self uprear,
To guard the lawful reasons on thy part:
   To leave poor me, thou hast the strength of laws,
   Since why to love I can allege no cause.

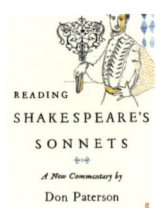

Reading Shakespeare's Sonnets by Don Paterson (2010)

JULY 2026

20 Monday

21 Tuesday

22 Wednesday

23 Thursday

24 Friday

25 Saturday 26 Sunday

JULY / AUGUST 2026

27 Monday

28 Tuesday

29 Wednesday

30 Thursday

31 Friday

1 Saturday   2 Sunday

SIMON ARMITAGE

Camera Obscura

This eight-year-old sitting in Bramhall's field,
shoes scuffed from kicking a stone,
too young for a key but old enough now
to walk the short mile back from school.

He's spied his mother down in the village
crossing the street, purse in her fist.
In her other hand her shopping bag nurses
four ugly potatoes caked in mud,

a boiling of peas, rags of meat or a tail of fish
in greaseproof paper, the price totted up
in pencilled columns of shillings and pence.
How warm must she be in that winter coat?

On Old Mount Road the nearer she gets
the smaller she shrinks, till he reaches out
to carry her home on the flat of his hand
or his fingertip, and she doesn't exist.

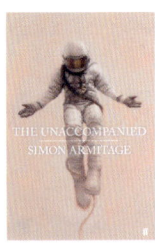

The Unaccompanied (2017)

AUGUST 2026

3 Monday AUGUST BANK HOLIDAY (SCT, IRL)

4 Tuesday

5 Wednesday

6 Thursday

7 Friday

8 Saturday

9 Sunday NATIONAL WOMEN'S DAY (ZA)

JOHN KEATS

The Human Seasons

Four Seasons fill the measure of the year;
    There are four seasons in the mind of man:
He has his lusty Spring, when fancy clear
    Takes in all beauty with an easy span:
He has his Summer, when luxuriously
    Spring's honied cud of youthful thought he loves
To ruminate, and by such dreaming high
    Is nearest unto heaven: quiet coves
His soul has in its Autumn, when his wings
    He furleth close; contented so to look
On mists in idleness – to let fair things
    Pass by unheeded as a threshold brook.
He has his Winter too of pale misfeature,
Or else he would forego his mortal nature.

POETRY PLEASE *The Seasons* (2015)

AUGUST 2026

10 Monday

11 Tuesday

12 Wednesday

13 Thursday

14 Friday

15 Saturday

16 Sunday

WALT WHITMAN

When I Heard the Learn'd Astronomer

When I heard the learn'd astronomer,
When the proofs, the figures, were ranged in columns before me,
When I was shown the charts and diagrams, to add, divide, and measure them,
When I sitting heard the astronomer where he lectured with much applause in the lecture-room,
How soon unaccountable I became tired and sick,
Till rising and gliding out I wander'd off by myself,
In the mystical moist night-air, and from time to time,
Look'd up in perfect silence at the stars.

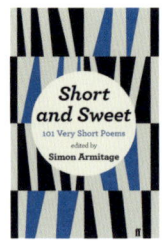

Short and Sweet (2002)

AUGUST 2026

17 Monday

18 Tuesday

19 Wednesday

20 Thursday

21 Friday

22 Saturday

23 Sunday

AUGUST 2026

24 Monday

25 Tuesday

26 Wednesday

27 Thursday

28 Friday

29 Saturday

30 Sunday

This in Land

That way a butterfly lifts an edge of world
is this horse chestnut tree going nowhere.

That way thunder feels bright and dark
is this moss, lit from under earth up.

That way the tip of a rosebud buries the future
is this stone smell unpronounced before rain.

That way a star's ground is mineral
is this steeple pointing down in the pond.

That way *this* ends, or doesn't with the word
is that way I am earthed by a hand.

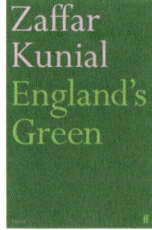

England's Green (2022)

AUGUST / SEPTEMBER 2026

31 **Monday**   SUMMER BANK HOLIDAY (UK, NOT SCT)

1 Tuesday

2 Wednesday

3 Thursday

4 Friday

5 Saturday   6 Sunday

WILLIAM WORDSWORTH

She dwelt among the untrodden ways

She dwelt among the untrodden ways
    Beside the springs of Dove,
A Maid whom there were none to praise
    And very few to love:

A violet by a mossy stone
    Half hidden from the eye!
— Fair as a star, when only one
    Is shining in the sky.

She lived unknown, and few could know
    When Lucy ceased to be;
But she is in her grave, and, oh,
    The difference to me!

POET TO POET *William Wordsworth: Poems Selected by Seamus Heaney* (2001)

SEPTEMBER 2026

7 Monday

8 Tuesday

9 Wednesday

10 Thursday

11 Friday

12 Saturday

13 Sunday

PHILIP LARKIN

Dublinesque

Down stucco sidestreets,
Where light is pewter
And afternoon mist
Brings lights on in shops
Above race-guides and rosaries,
A funeral passes.

The hearse is ahead,
But after there follows
A troop of streetwalkers
In wide flowered hats,
Leg-of-mutton sleeves,
And ankle-length dresses.

There is an air of great friendliness,
As if they were honouring
One they were fond of;
Some caper a few steps,
Skirts held skilfully
(Someone claps time),

And of great sadness also.
As they wend away
A voice is heard singing
Of Kitty, or Katy,
As if the name meant once
All love, all beauty.

The Complete Poems (2012)

SEPTEMBER 2026

14 Monday

15 Tuesday

16 Wednesday

17 Thursday

18 Friday

19 Saturday

20 Sunday

The Lake Isle of Innisfree

I will arise and go now, and go to Innisfree,
And a small cabin build there, of clay and wattles made:
Nine bean-rows will I have there, a hive for the honey-bee,
And live alone in the bee-loud glade.

And I shall have some peace there, for peace comes dropping slow,
Dropping from the veils of the morning to where the cricket sings;
There midnight's all a glimmer, and noon a purple glow,
And evening full of the linnet's wings.

I will arise and go now, for always night and day
I hear lake water lapping with low sounds by the shore;
While I stand on the roadway, or on the pavements grey,
I hear it in the deep heart's core.

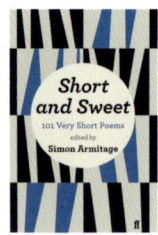

Short and Sweet (2002)

SEPTEMBER 2026

21 Monday

22 Tuesday

23 Wednesday

24 Thursday   HERITAGE DAY (ZA)

25 Friday

26 Saturday

27 Sunday

ANDREW MOTION

September / October 2026

28 Monday

29 Tuesday

30 Wednesday

1 Thursday   NATIONAL POETRY DAY (UK)

2 Friday

3 Saturday

4 Sunday

GEORGE BARKER

LVIII

The children are gone. The holiday is over.
Outside it is Fall. Inside it is so
quiet that the silence seems inclined to
talk to itself. They will not recover
the summer of seventy-seven again, even
though they become, in turn, their own children.

I sit in my sixty odd years and wonder
how often before in this old house a man has
sat thinking of what is now, and what was.
But can it serve a serious purpose to ponder
upon the imponderable? There, there beyond a
fall glimmers the long-lost garden.

That garden where we, too, as in a spell
stared eye into dazed eye and did not see
that suddenly the holy day was over,
the flashing lifeguard, the worm in the tree,
the glittering of the bright sword as it fell,
and the gate closing for all time to be.

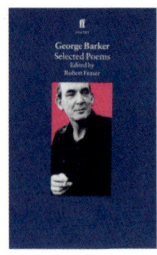

Selected Poems (1995)

OCTOBER 2026

5 Monday

6 Tuesday

7 Wednesday

8 Thursday

9 Friday

10 Saturday   11 Sunday

TED HUGHES

Littleblood

O littleblood, hiding from the mountains in the mountains
Wounded by stars and leaking shadow
Eating the medical earth.

O littleblood, little boneless little skinless
Ploughing with a linnet's carcase
Reaping the wind and threshing the stones.

O littleblood, drumming in a cow's skull
Dancing with a gnat's feet
With an elephant's nose with a crocodile's tail.

Grown so wise grown so terrible
Sucking death's mouldy tits.

Sit on my finger, sing in my ear, O littleblood.

Collected Poems (2005)

OCTOBER 2026

12 Monday

13 Tuesday

14 Wednesday

15 Thursday

16 Friday

17 Saturday   18 Sunday

STEVIE SMITH

Forgive me, forgive me

Forgive me forgive me my heart is my own
And not to be given for any man's frown
Yet would I not keep it for ever alone.

Forgive me forgive me I thought that I loved
My fancy betrayed me my heart was unmoved
My fancy too often has carelessly roved.

Forgive me forgive me for here where I stand
There is no friend beside me no lover at hand
No footstep but mine in my desert of sand.

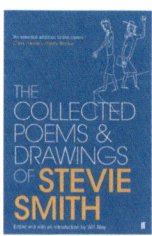

The Collected Poems & Drawings (2015)

OCTOBER 2026

19 Monday

20 Tuesday

21 Wednesday

22 Thursday

23 Friday

24 Saturday   25 Sunday

JULIA COPUS

Stories

Think of a night in midsummer, a night with water
falling to a pond from the raised mouth

of a freckled stone seal, & children up late
calling to each other two or three gardens away, & under

those a softer murmur. So lies the past,
no further. You do not need to get up

& stand on tiptoe at the hedge to know
that what you hear are the people you love. You suppose

the stories I've told are over. Think of the garden.
You sat there so long the dew had settled

on the grass, on the yellow pistils of the irises, the
    children's hair.
Their laughter was made of the same

air that moved as a breeze across you, & the dew likewise
was bits of sky, nestling where it could, & all of it

(although you could not touch it)
was part of you, was what the summer night contained.

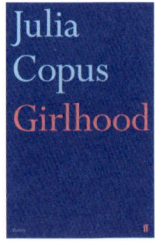

Girlhood (2019)

OCTOBER / NOVEMBER 2026

26 Monday LABOUR DAY (NZ)
           OCTOBER BANK HOLIDAY (IRL)

27 Tuesday

28 Wednesday

29 Thursday

30 Friday

31 Saturday HALLOWEEN   1 Sunday

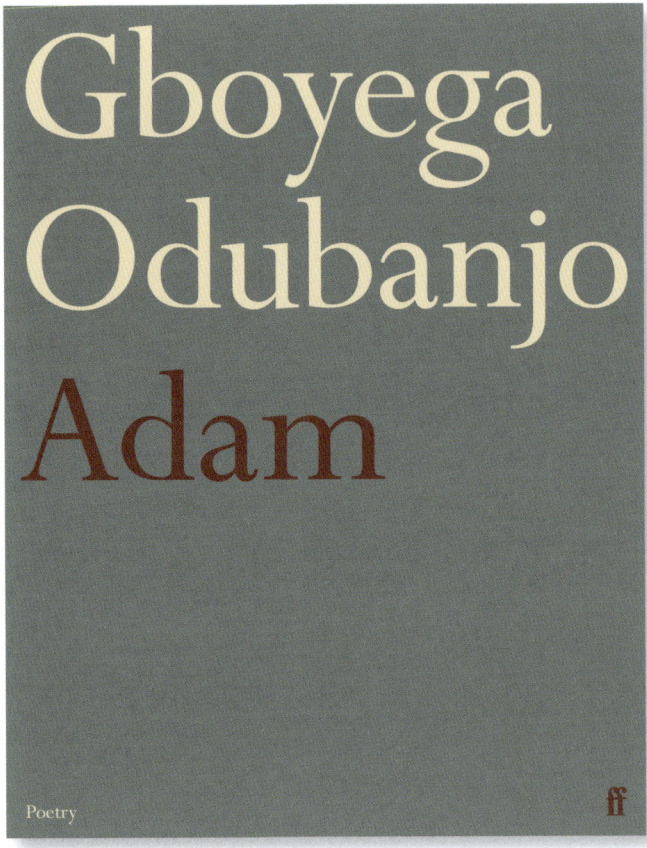

NOVEMBER 2026

2 Monday

3 Tuesday

4 Wednesday

5 Thursday

6 Friday

7 Saturday

8 Sunday — REMEMBRANCE SUNDAY

Firing Squad

On balconies, sunlight. On poplars, sunlight, on our lips.
Today no one is shooting.
A girl cuts her hair with imaginary scissors —
the scissors in sunlight, her hair in sunlight.
Another girl nicks a pair of shoes from a sleeping soldier, skewered
    with light.
As soldiers wake and gape at us gaping at them,
what do they see?
Tonight they shot fifty women on Lerna Street.
I sit down to write and tell you what I know:
a child learns the world by putting it in her mouth,
a girl becomes a woman and a woman, earth.
Body, they blame you for all things and they
seek in the body what does not live in the body.

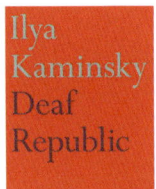

Deaf Republic (2019)

NOVEMBER 2026

9 Monday

10 Tuesday

11 Wednesday REMEMBRANCE DAY

12 Thursday

13 Friday

14 Saturday

15 Sunday

SYLVIA PLATH

Crossing the Water

Black lake, black boat, two black, cut-paper people.
Where do the black trees go that drink here?
Their shadows must cover Canada.

A little light is filtering from the water flowers.
Their leaves do not wish us to hurry:
They are round and flat and full of dark advice.

Cold worlds shake from the oar.
The spirit of blackness is in us, it is in the fishes.
A snag is lifting a valedictory, pale hand;

Stars open among the lilies.
Are you not blinded by such expressionless sirens?
This is the silence of astounded souls.

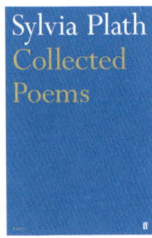

Collected Poems (1981)

NOVEMBER 2026

16 Monday

17 Tuesday

18 Wednesday

19 Thursday

20 Friday

21 Saturday   22 Sunday

Sisu

To persevere in hope of summer.
To adapt to its broken promise.
To love winter.

To sleep.

To love winter.
To adapt to its broken promise.
To persevere in hope of summer.

Selected Poems (2024)

NOVEMBER 2026

23 Monday

24 Tuesday

25 Wednesday

26 Thursday

27 Friday

28 Saturday					29 Sunday

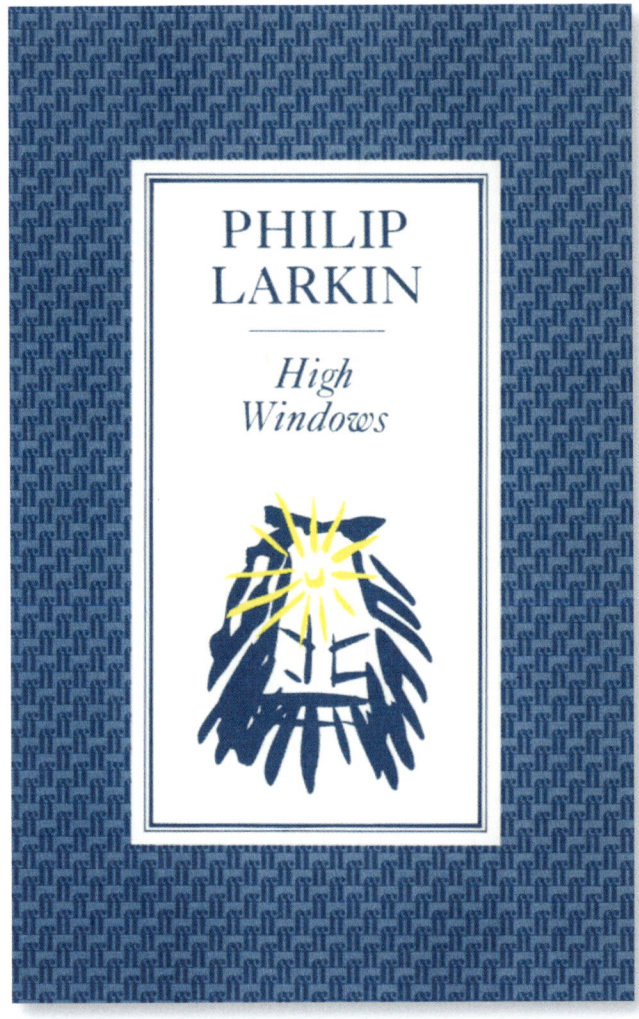

NOVEMBER / DECEMBER 2026

30 Monday   ST ANDREW'S DAY HOLIDAY (SCT)

1 Tuesday

2 Wednesday

3 Thursday

4 Friday

5 Saturday

6 Sunday

GERARD MANLEY HOPKINS

Peace

When will you ever, Peace, wild wooddove, shy wings shut,
Your round me roaming end, and under be my boughs?
When, when, Peace, will you, Peace? – I'll not play hypocrite

To own my heart: I yield you do come sometimes; but
That piecemeal peace is poor peace. What pure peace allows
Alarms of wars, the daunting wars, the death of it?

O surely, reaving Peace, my Lord should leave in lieu
Some good! And so he does leave Patience exquisite,
That plumes to Peace thereafter. And when Peace here does house
He comes with work to do, he does not come to coo,
            He comes to brood and sit.

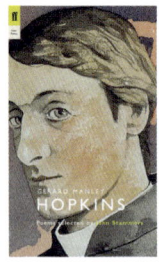

POET TO POET *Gerard Manley Hopkins: Poems Selected by John Stammers* (2012)

DECEMBER 2026

7 Monday

8 Tuesday

9 Wednesday

10 Thursday

11 Friday

12 Saturday

13 Sunday

PERCY BYSSHE SHELLEY

Ozymandias

I met a traveller from an antique land
Who said: Two vast and trunkless legs of stone
Stand in the desert. Near them on the sand,
Half sunk, a shatter'd visage lies, whose frown
And wrinkled lip and sneer of cold command
Tell that its sculptor well those passions read
Which yet survive, stamp'd on these lifeless things,
The hand that mock'd them and the heart that fed;
And on the pedestal these words appear:
'My name is Ozymandias, king of kings:
Look on my works, ye Mighty, and despair!'
Nothing beside remains. Round the decay
Of that colossal wreck, boundless and bare,
The lone and level sands stretch far away.

The Rattle Bag (2005)

DECEMBER 2026

14 Monday

15 Tuesday

16 Wednesday DAY OF RECONCILIATION (ZA)

17 Thursday

18 Friday

19 Saturday   20 Sunday

THOMAS HARDY

The House of Hospitalities

Here we broached the Christmas barrel,
    Pushed up the charred log-ends;
Here we sang the Christmas carol,
    And called in friends.

Time has tired me since we met here
    When the folk now dead were young,
Since the viands were outset here
    And quaint songs sung.

And the worm has bored the viol
    That used to lead the tune,
Rust eaten out the dial
    That struck night's noon.

Now no Christmas brings in neighbours,
    And the New Year comes unlit;
Where we sang the mole now labours,
    And spiders knit.

Yet at midnight if here walking,
    When the moon sheets wall and tree,
I see forms of old time talking,
    Who smile on me.

POET TO POET *Thomas Hardy: Poems Selected by Tom Paulin* (2001)

DECEMBER 2026

21 Monday

22 Tuesday

23 Wednesday

24 Thursday   CHRISTMAS EVE

25 Friday   CHRISTMAS DAY (UK, IRL, AUS, ZA, NZ)

26 Saturday   BOXING DAY / DAY OF GOODWILL / ST STEPHEN'S DAY (ZA)

27 Sunday

THE POETRY OF W.B. YEATS

BY LOUIS MACNEICE

With a Foreword by Richard Ellmann

DECEMBER 2026 / JANUARY 2027

28 Monday   BOXING DAY HOLIDAY (UK, IRL, AUS, NZ)

29 Tuesday

30 Wednesday

31 Thursday   NEW YEAR'S EVE

1 Friday   NEW YEAR'S DAY (UK, AUS, ZA, NZ)

2 Saturday   DAY AFTER NEW YEAR'S DAY (NZ)

3 Sunday

A Brief Chronology of Faber's Poetry Publishing

1925 Geoffrey Faber acquires an interest in The Scientific Press and renames the firm Faber and Gwyer. ¶ The poet/bank clerk T. S. Eliot is recruited. 'What will impress my directors favourably is the sense that in you we have found a man who combines literary gifts with business instincts' – Geoffrey Faber to T. S. Eliot ¶ Eliot brought with him *The Criterion*, the quarterly periodical he had been editing since 1922. (*The Waste Land* had appeared in its first issue, brilliantly establishing its reputation.) He continued to edit it from the Faber offices until it closed in 1939. Though unprofitable, it was hugely influential, introducing early work by Auden, Empson and Spender, among others, and promoting many notable European writers, including Proust and Valéry. ¶ Publication of T. S. Eliot's *Poems, 1909–1925*, which included *The Waste Land* and a new sequence, *The Hollow Men*. ¶

1927 From 1927 to 1931 Faber publishes a series of illustrated pamphlets known as *The Ariel Poems* containing unpublished poems by an eminent poet (Thomas Hardy, W. B. Yeats, Harold Monro, Edith Sitwell and Edmund Blunden, to name but a few) along with an illustration, usually in colour, by a leading contemporary artist (including Eric Gill, Eric Ravilious, Paul Nash and Graham Sutherland). ¶

1928 Faber and Gwyer announce the *Selected Poems of Ezra Pound*, with an introduction and notes by Eliot. ¶

1929 Geoffrey Faber buys out Lady Gwyer and oversees the birth of the Faber and Faber imprint. Legend has it that Walter de la Mare, the father of Faber director Richard de la Mare, suggested the euphonious repetition: another Faber in the company name 'because you can't have too much of a good thing'. ¶

1930 W. H. Auden becomes a Faber poet with a collection entitled simply *Poems*. ¶ Eliot publishes *Ash Wednesday*. ¶

1933 Stephen Spender becomes a Faber poet with his first collection *Poems*, a companion piece to Auden's 1930 work of the same name. ¶ The first British edition of James Joyce's *Pomes Penyeach* is published. ¶

1935 The American poet Marianne Moore publishes with Faber. 'Miss Moore's poems form part of a small body of durable poetry written in our time' – T. S. Eliot ¶ Louis MacNeice becomes a Faber poet. 'The most original Irish poet of his generation' – Faber catalogue 1935 ¶

1936 The hugely influential *Faber Book of Modern Verse* (edited by Michael Roberts) is published. ¶

1937 *In Parenthesis* by David Jones is published. 'This is an epic of war. But it is like no other war-book because for the first time that experience has been reduced to "a shape in words." The impression still remains that this book is one of the most remarkable literary achievements of our time' — *Times Literary Supplement* ¶ W. H. Auden is awarded the Queen's Gold Medal for Poetry. ¶

1939 T. S. Eliot's *Old Possum's Book of Practical Cats* is published with a book jacket illustrated by the author. Originally called *Pollicle Dogs and Jellicle Cats*, the poems were written for his five godchildren. The eldest of these was Geoffrey Faber's son Tom — himself much later a director of Faber and Faber. ¶

1944 Walter de la Mare's *Peacock Pie* is published with illustrations by Edward Ardizzone. ¶

1947 Philip Larkin's first novel, *A Girl in Winter*, is published. 'A young man with an exceptionally clear sense of what, as a writer, he means to do' — *Times Literary Supplement* ¶

1948 T. S. Eliot wins the Nobel Prize in Literature. ¶

1949 Ezra Pound's *Pisan Cantos* is published. 'The most incomprehensible passages are often more stimulating than much comprehensibility which passes for poetry today' — *Times Literary Supplement* ¶

1954 *The Ariel Poems* are revived with a new set of pamphlets by W. H. Auden, Stephen Spender, Louis MacNeice, T. S. Eliot, Walter de la Mare, Cecil Day Lewis and Roy Campbell. The artists include Edward Ardizzone, Edward Bawden, Michael Ayrton and John Piper. ¶

1957 Ted Hughes comes to Faber with *The Hawk in the Rain*. ¶ Siegfried Sassoon receives the Queen's Gold Medal for Poetry. ¶

1959 Robert Lowell's collection *Life Studies* is published. ¶

1960 Saint-John Perse wins the Nobel Prize in Literature. ¶

1961 Geoffrey Faber dies. ¶ Ted Hughes's first collection of children's poems, *Meet My Folks*, is published. ¶

1963 The Geoffrey Faber Memorial Prize is established as an annual prize awarded in alternating years to a single volume of poetry or fiction by a Commonwealth author under forty. ¶

1964 Philip Larkin's *The Whitsun Weddings* is published. ¶

1965 T. S. Eliot dies. ¶ Sylvia Plath's posthumous collection, *Ariel*, is published. 'Her extraordinary achievement, poised as she was between volatile emotional state and the edge of the precipice' – Frieda Hughes ¶ Philip Larkin is awarded the Queen's Gold Medal for Poetry. ¶

1966 Seamus Heaney comes to Faber with *Death of a Naturalist*. ¶ Sylvia Plath's novel *The Bell Jar* is published by Faber. ¶

1968 Ted Hughes's *The Iron Man* is published. ¶

1971 Stephen Spender is awarded the Queen's Gold Medal for Poetry. ¶

1973 Paul Muldoon comes to Faber with his first collection, *New Weather*. ¶

1974 Ted Hughes receives the Queen's Gold Medal for Poetry. ¶

1977 Tom Paulin comes to Faber with his first collection, *A State of Justice*. ¶ Norman Nicholson receives the Queen's Gold Medal for Poetry. ¶

1980 Czesław Miłosz wins the Nobel Prize in Literature. ¶

1981 *Cats*, the Andrew Lloyd Webber musical based on *Old Possum's Book of Practical Cats*, opens in London. ¶

1984 *Rich*, a collection by Faber's own poetry editor, Craig Raine, is published. 'Puts us in touch with life as unexpectedly and joyfully as early Pasternak' – John Bayley ¶ Ted Hughes becomes Poet Laureate. ¶

1985 Douglas Dunn's collection *Elegies* is the Whitbread Book of the Year. ¶

1986 Vikram Seth's *The Golden Gate* is published. ¶

1987 Seamus Heaney's *The Haw Lantern* wins the Whitbread Poetry Award. ¶

1988 Derek Walcott is awarded the Queen's Gold Medal for Poetry. ¶

1992 Derek Walcott wins the Nobel Prize in Literature. ¶ Thom Gunn's collection *The Man with the Night Sweats* wins the Forward Poetry Prize for Best Collection, while Simon Armitage's *Kid* wins Best First Collection. ¶

1993 Andrew Motion wins the Whitbread Biography Award for his book on Philip Larkin. ¶ Don Paterson's *Nil Nil* wins the Forward Poetry Prize for Best First Collection. ¶

1994 Paul Muldoon wins the T. S. Eliot Prize for *The Annals of Chile*. ¶ Alice Oswald wins an Eric Gregory Award. ¶

1995 Seamus Heaney wins the Nobel Prize in Literature. ¶

1996 Wisława Szymborska wins the Nobel Prize in Literature. ¶ Seamus Heaney's *The Spirit Level* wins the Whitbread Book of the Year Award. 'Touched by a sense of wonder' – Blake Morrison ¶

1997 Don Paterson wins the T. S. Eliot Prize for *God's Gift to Women*. ¶ Lavinia Greenlaw wins the Forward Prize for Best Single Poem for 'A World Where News Travelled Slowly'. ¶ Ted Hughes's *Tales from Ovid* is the Whitbread Book of the Year. 'A breathtaking book' – John Carey ¶

1998 Ted Hughes wins the Whitbread Book of the Year for the second time running with *Birthday Letters*, which also wins the T. S. Eliot Prize. 'Language like lava, its molten turmoils hardening into jagged shapes' – John Carey ¶ Ted Hughes is awarded the Order of Merit. ¶ Christopher Logue receives the Wilfred Owen Poetry Award. ¶

1999 Seamus Heaney's *Beowulf* wins the Whitbread Book of the Year Award. '[Heaney is the] one living poet who can rightly claim to be Beowulf's heir' – *New York Times* ¶ A memorial service for Ted Hughes is held at Westminster Abbey. In his speech Seamus Heaney calls Hughes 'a guardian spirit of the land and language'. ¶ Hugo Williams wins the T. S. Eliot Prize for his collection *Billy's Rain*. ¶ Andrew Motion is appointed Poet Laureate. ¶

2000 Seamus Heaney receives the Wilfred Owen Poetry Award. ¶

2002 Alice Oswald wins the T. S. Eliot Prize for Poetry for her collection *Dart*. ¶

2003 Paul Muldoon is awarded the Pulitzer Prize for Poetry for *Moy Sand and Gravel*. *Landing Light* by Don Paterson wins the Whitbread Poetry Award. ¶

2004 August Kleinzahler receives the International Griffin Poetry Prize for *The Strange Hours Travellers Keep*. ¶ Hugo Williams is awarded the Queen's Gold Medal for Poetry. ¶

2005 David Harsent wins the Forward Prize for Best Collection for *Legion*. ¶ Harold Pinter receives the Wilfred Owen Poetry Award. ¶ Charles Simic receives the International Griffin Poetry Prize for *Selected Poems 1963–2003*. ¶ Nick Laird wins an Eric Gregory Award. ¶

2006 Christopher Logue wins the Whitbread Poetry Award for *Cold Calls*. ¶ The Geoffrey Faber Memorial Prize is awarded to Alice Oswald for *Woods Etc.* ¶ Seamus Heaney wins the T. S. Eliot Prize for *District and Circle*. ¶

2007 Tony Harrison is awarded the Wilfred Owen Poetry Award. ¶ Daljit Nagra wins the Forward Prize for Best First Collection for *Look We Have Coming to Dover!* ¶ James Fenton receives the Queen's Gold Medal for Poetry. ¶

2008 Daljit Nagra wins the South Bank Show / Arts Council Decibel Award. ¶ Mick Imlah's collection *The Lost Leader* wins the Forward Prize for Best Collection. ¶

2009 Carol Ann Duffy becomes Poet Laureate. ¶ Don Paterson's *Rain* wins the Forward Poetry Prize for Best Collection, while *The Striped World* by Emma Jones wins the Best First Collection Prize. ¶ The Queen's Gold Medal for Poetry is awarded to Don Paterson. ¶

2010 *The Song of Lunch* by Christopher Reid is shortlisted for the Ted Hughes Award for New Work in Poetry and he is awarded the Costa Poetry Award for *A Scattering*. ¶ The John Florio Prize for Italian Translation 2010 is awarded to Jamie McKendrick for *The Embrace*. ¶ Derek Walcott wins both the Warwick Prize and the T. S. Eliot Prize for Poetry for his collection *White Egrets*. ¶ *Rain* by Don Paterson is shortlisted for the Saltire Scottish Book of the Year. ¶ Tony Harrison is awarded the Prix Européen de Littérature. ¶ The Keats–Shelley Prize is awarded to Simon Armitage for his poem 'The Present'. ¶ The Forward Prize for Best Collection is awarded to Seamus Heaney for *Human Chain*. ¶ Also shortlisted for the Forward Prize for Best Collection are Lachlan Mackinnon for *Small Hours* and Jo Shapcott for *Of Mutability*. ¶ The Centre for Literacy in Primary Education (CLPE) Poetry Prize is awarded to Carol Ann Duffy for *New and Collected Poems for Children*. ¶ Alice Oswald wins the Ted Hughes Award for New Work in Poetry for *Weeds and Wild Flowers*. ¶ *The Striped World* by Emma Jones is shortlisted for the Adelaide Festival Poetry Award. ¶ The Queen's Gold Medal for Poetry is awarded to Gillian Clarke. ¶

2011 *Of Mutability* by Jo Shapcott is the Costa Book of the Year. ¶ *Human Chain* by Seamus Heaney and *Maggot* by Paul Muldoon are both shortlisted for the *Irish Times* Poetry Now Award. ¶ *Night* by David Harsent is shortlisted for the Forward Prize for Best Collection. ¶ 'Bees' by Jo Shapcott is shortlisted for the Forward Prize for Best Single Poem. ¶ A new digital edition of T. S. Eliot's *The Waste Land* for iPad is launched, bringing to life one of the most revolutionary poems of the last hundred years, illuminated by a wealth of interactive features. ¶ The Queen's Gold Medal for Poetry is awarded to Jo Shapcott. ¶ At Westminster Abbey a memorial is dedicated to Ted Hughes in Poets' Corner. ¶

2012 *The Death of King Arthur* by Simon Armitage is shortlisted for the T. S. Eliot Prize. ¶ *The World's Two Smallest Humans* by Julia Copus is shortlisted for the T. S. Eliot Prize and the Costa Poetry Award. ¶ David Harsent's collection *Night* wins the International Griffin Poetry Prize. ¶ *81 Austerities* by Sam Riviere wins the Felix Dennis Prize for Best First Collection, one of the Forward Prizes for Poetry. ¶ *Farmers Cross* by Bernard O'Donoghue is shortlisted for the *Irish Times* Poetry Now Award. ¶

2013 The Forward Prize for Best First Collection is awarded to Emily Berry for *Dear Boy*. ¶ Hugo Williams is shortlisted for the Forward Prize for Best Single Poem for 'From the Dialysis Ward'. ¶ Alice Oswald is awarded the Warwick Prize for Writing for her collection *Memorial*, which also wins the Poetry Society's Corneliu M. Popescu Prize for poetry in translation. ¶ The Queen's Gold Medal for Poetry is awarded to Douglas Dunn. ¶ The shortlist for the T. S. Eliot Prize includes Daljit Nagra for *The Ramayana: A Retelling* and Maurice Riordan for *The Water Stealer*. ¶ *Pink Mist* by Owen Sheers wins the Hay Festival Medal for Poetry. ¶ In his eulogy for Seamus Heaney, Paul Muldoon says, 'We remember the beauty of Seamus Heaney – as a bard, and in his being.' In November the first official tribute evenings to Heaney are held at Harvard, then in New York, followed by events at the Royal Festival Hall in London, the Waterfront Hall, Belfast, and the Sheldonian, Oxford. ¶

2014 Maurice Riordan is shortlisted for the Pigott Poetry Prize for *The Water Stealer*. ¶ Hugo Williams is shortlisted for the Forward Prize for Best Collection for *I Knew the Bride*. ¶ Daljit Nagra is awarded the Society of Authors Travelling Scholarship. ¶ Nick Laird's *Go Giants* is shortlisted for the *Irish Times* Poetry Now Award. ¶ Emily Berry, Emma Jones and Daljit Nagra are announced as three of the Poetry Book Society's Next Generation Poets 2014. ¶ *Pink Mist* by Owen Sheers is named the Wales Book of the Year after winning the poetry category. ¶

2015 *Fire Songs* by David Harsent is awarded the T. S. Eliot Prize for Poetry. ¶ Alice Oswald wins the Ted Hughes Award for New Work for *Tithonus*, a poem and performance commissioned by London's Southbank Centre. ¶ *One Thousand Things Worth Knowing* by Paul Muldoon wins the Pigott Poetry Prize. ¶ Don Paterson is awarded the Neustadt International Prize for Literature. ¶ *Terror* by Toby Martinez de las Rivas is shortlisted for the Seamus Heaney Centre for Poetry's Prize for First Full Collection. ¶ Paul Muldoon's *One Thousand Things Worth Knowing* is shortlisted for the Forward Prize for Best Collection. ¶ James Fenton is awarded the Pen Pinter Prize. ¶ *40 Sonnets* by Don Paterson wins the Costa Poetry Award, and is shortlisted for the T. S. Eliot Prize. ¶

2016 Don Paterson is shortlisted for the International Griffin Poetry Prize. ¶ *40 Sonnets* by Don Paterson is shortlisted for the Saltire Society Literary Awards. ¶ *The Seasons of Cullen Church* by Bernard O'Donoghue is shortlisted for the T. S. Eliot Prize. ¶ Jack Underwood receives a Somerset Maugham Award. ¶ An excerpt from *Salt* by David Harsent is shortlisted for the Forward Prize for Best Single Poem. ¶

2017 *The Unaccompanied* by Simon Armitage, *Stranger, Baby* by Emily Berry and *The Noise of a Fly* by Douglas Dunn all receive Recommendations from the Poetry Book Society. They also give a Special Commendation to *Selected Poems of Thom*

Gunn, edited by Clive Wilmer. ¶ Simon Armitage receives the PEN Award for Poetry in Translation for *Pearl*. ¶ Bernard O'Donoghue's collection *The Seasons of Cullen Church* is shortlisted for the Pigott Poetry Prize. ¶ Emily Berry's collection *Stranger, Baby* is shortlisted for the Forward Prize for Best Collection. ¶ Sam Riviere's collection *Kim Kardashian's Marriage* is shortlisted for the Ledbury Poetry Prize. ¶ Douglas Dunn's collection *The Noise of a Fly* is shortlisted for the T. S. Eliot Prize. ¶ Paul Muldoon is awarded the Queen's Gold Medal for Poetry. ¶

2018 Matthew Francis's collection *The Mabinogi* is shortlisted for the Ted Hughes Award and Welsh Book of the Year. ¶ Toby Martinez de las Rivas's collection *Black Sun* is shortlisted for the Forward Prize for Best Collection. ¶ Richard Scott's collection *Soho* is shortlisted for the Forward Prize for Best First Collection, the T. S. Eliot Prize and the Costa Poetry Award. ¶ Owen Sheers is the recipient of the Wilfred Owen Poetry Award for 2018. ¶ Daljit Nagra receives a Society of Authors Cholmondeley Award. ¶ Seamus Heaney's collection *100 Poems* is shortlisted for the 2018 Books Are My Bag Readers Awards, Poetry category. ¶ Nick Laird's collection *Feel Free* is shortlisted for the T. S. Eliot Prize. ¶ Zaffar Kunial's collection *Us* is shortlisted for the Costa Poetry Award and the T. S. Eliot Prize. ¶ Hannah Sullivan's collection *Three Poems* is shortlisted for the Roehampton Poetry Prize and the Costa Poetry Award, and goes on to win the T. S. Eliot Prize. ¶ Simon Armitage is awarded the Queen's Gold Medal for Poetry. ¶

2019 Simon Armitage is appointed Poet Laureate. ¶ Richard Scott's collection *Soho* is shortlisted for the Roehampton Poetry Prize and the Polari First Book Prize. ¶ Hannah Sullivan's collection *Three Poems* wins the John Pollard Foundation International Poetry Prize and is shortlisted for the Ted Hughes Award, the Seamus Heaney First Collection Prize and the Michael Murphy Memorial Prize. ¶ Sophie Collins's collection *Who Is Mary Sue?* is shortlisted for the 2018 Saltire Society's Scottish Poetry Book of the Year and wins both the Michael Murphy Memorial Prize and an Eric Gregory Award. ¶ Ishion Hutchinson's collection *House of Lords and Commons* wins the Windham-Campbell Prize. ¶ Lavinia Greenlaw's collection *The Built Moment* is shortlisted for the Roehampton Poetry Prize and the East Anglian Book Award (poetry category). ¶ Zaffar Kunial's collection *Us* is shortlisted for the 2019 Rathbones Folio Prize, the Roehampton Poetry Prize and the Michael Murphy Memorial Prize. ¶ 'The Window' from Mary Jean Chan's collection *Flèche* is shortlisted for the Forward Prize for Best Single Poem and her poem 'The Fencer' wins the Geoffrey Dearmer Prize. ¶ Poems from Rachael Allen, Lavinia Greenlaw, Paul Muldoon and Hugo Williams are Highly Commended for the Forward Prizes for Poetry. ¶ Ilya Kaminsky's collection *Deaf Republic* is shortlisted for the Forward Prize for Best Collection, the T. S. Eliot Prize and the US National Book Award (poetry category). ¶

2020 Mary Jean Chan's collection *Flèche* wins the Costa Poetry Award and is shortlisted for both the John Pollard International Poetry Prize and the Seamus Heaney First Collection Poetry Prize. ¶ Nick Laird's collection *Feel Free* is shortlisted for the Derek Walcott Poetry Prize. ¶ Julia Copus's collection *Girlhood* is shortlisted for the Derek Walcott Poetry Prize. ¶ Paul Muldoon's collection *Frolic and Detour* is shortlisted for the *Irish Times* Poetry Now Award. ¶ Natalie Diaz's collection *Postcolonial Love Poem* is shortlisted for the T. S. Eliot Prize and the US National Book Award (poetry category). ¶

2021 Natalie Diaz's collection *Postcolonial Love Poem* wins the Pulitzer Prize for Poetry, is a finalist for the Neustadt International Prize for Literature and *LA Times* Prize for Poetry, and is longlisted for the Laurel Prize. ¶ Jack Underwood's collection *A Year in the New Life* is shortlisted for the T. S. Eliot Prize. ¶ Barbara Kingsolver's collection *How to Fly* is longlisted for the Laurel Prize. ¶ Mary Jean Chan's collection *Flèche* is a finalist for the LAMBDA Award for Lesbian Poetry. ¶ The Derek Walcott Prize for Poetry shortlist includes Simon Armitage's collection *Magnetic Field*; David Harsent's collection *Loss*; Andrew Motion's collection *Randomly Moving Particles*; Don Paterson's collection *Zonal*; and Christopher Reid's collection *The Late Sun*. ¶ Maurice Riordan's collection *Shoulder Tap* is shortlisted for the Pigott Poetry Prize. ¶ Paul Muldoon's collection *Howdie-Skelp* is shortlisted for the Pigott Poetry Prize. ¶

2022 Nidhi Zak/Aria Eipe's collection *Auguries of a Minor God* is shortlisted for the John Pollard Prize and the Dylan Thomas Prize. ¶ Jack Underwood's collection *A Year in the New Life* and Emily Berry's collection *Unexhausted Time* are longlisted for the Laurel Prize. ¶ Zaffar Kunial's collection *England's Green* is shortlisted for the T. S. Eliot Prize. ¶ Victoria Adukwei Bulley's collection *Quiet* is shortlisted for the T. S. Eliot Prize. ¶ 'Up Late' by Nick Laird wins the Forward Prize for Best Single Poem. ¶ Simon Armitage's collection *The Owl and the Nightingale* is shortlisted for the Derek Walcott Prize. ¶

2023 Victoria Adukwei Bulley's collection *Quiet* wins the John Pollard Prize for Poetry and the Rathbone Folio Prize for Poetry. ¶ Mary Jean Chan's collection *Bright Fear* is shortlisted for the Forward Prize for Best Collection. ¶ Zaffar Kunial's collection *England's Green* is shortlisted for the Rathbones Folio Prize for Poetry, the Ondaatje Prize and the Ledbury Hellens Prize for a Second

Collection and is runner-up for the Laurel Prize. ¶ Don Paterson's collection *The Arctic* is longlisted for the Laurel Prize. ¶ Ishion Hutchinson's collection *School of Instructions* is shortlisted for the T. S. Eliot Prize. ¶ Daljit Nagra's collection *Indiom* is a Poetry Book Society Choice for 2023. ¶

2024 Ishion Hutchinson's collection *School of Instructions* is shortlisted for the Griffith Poetry Prize. ¶ Declan Ryan's collection *Crisis Actor* is shortlisted for the John Pollard International Poetry Prize. ¶ Mary Jean Chan's collection *Bright Fear* is shortlisted for the Dylan Thomas Prize. ¶ Rachael Allen's collection *God Complex* is shortlisted for the Forward Prize – Best Collection. ¶ Ishion Hutchinson's Section XXVIII of *School of Instructions* is Highly Commended by the Forward Prize. ¶ Christopher Reid's collection *Toys / Tricks / Traps*, Nick Laird's collection *Up Late* and Hannah Sullivan's collection *Was It for This* are shortlisted for the Derek Walcott Prize. ¶ Gboyega Odubanjo's collection *Adam* is shortlisted for the T. S. Eliot Prize. ¶

Acknowledgements

Poetry

'Mozart in the Shopping Centre' taken from *Collected Poems 1973–2023* © Wendy Cope ¶ 'Wind' taken from *The Green Month* © Matthew Francis ¶ 'The Supreme Being alone' taken from *Ramayana* © Daljit Nagra ¶ 'from Ars Poetica XI' taken from *Bright Fear* © Mary Jean Chan ¶ 'Miracle' taken from *New Selected Poems 1988–2013* © The Estate of Seamus Heaney ¶ 'dear little b,' taken from *Quiet* © Victoria Adukwei Bulley ¶ 'Cadfannan' taken from *The Gododdin* © Gillian Clarke ¶ 'An Unexpected Meeting' taken from *Poems New and Collected 1957–1997* © Wisława Szymborska, translated from the Polish by Stanisław Barańczak and Clare Cavanagh, English translation © 1998 by Harcourt Brace & Company ¶ 'True Happy Stories' taken from *The Missing Months* © Lachlan Mackinnon ¶ 'To My Guitarist' taken from *Foxglovewise* © Ange Mlinko ¶ 'Dormitory' taken from *The Poetry of Derek Walcott 1948–2013* © The Estate of Derek Walcott ¶ 'Red Jasper' taken from *That Broke into Shining Crystals* © Richard Scott ¶ 'Preludes IV' taken from *Collected Poems 1909–1962* © Set Copyrights Limited ¶ 'After George Herbert' taken from *After You Were, I Am* © Camille Ralphs ¶ 'Crossing the Water' taken from *Collected Poems* © The Estate of Sylvia Plath ¶ 'Song' taken from *Stranger, Baby* © Emily Berry ¶ 'L' taken from *School of Instructions* © Ishion Hutchinson ¶ 'Sisu' taken from *Selected Poems* © Lavinia Greenlaw ¶ 'Camera Obscura' taken from *The Unaccompanied* © Simon Armitage ¶ 'This in Land' taken from *England's Green* © Zaffar Kunial ¶ 'Dublinesque' taken from *The Complete Poems* (2012) © The Estate of Philip Larkin ¶ 'LVIII' taken from *Selected Poems* © The Estate of George Barker ¶ 'Littleblood' taken from *Collected Poems* © The Estate of Ted Hughes ¶ 'Forgive me, forgive me' taken from *Collected Poems and Drawings* © The Estate of Stevie Smith ¶ 'Stories' taken from *Girlhood* © Julia Copus ¶ 'Firing Squad' taken from *Deaf Republic* © Ilya Kaminsky ¶ 'Crossing the Water' taken from *Collected Poems* © The Estate of Sylvia Plath

All poetry reprinted by permission of Faber & Faber unless otherwise stated.

Picture credits

Jack Straw's Castle by Thom Gunn, design by Berthold Wolpe
Joy in Service on Rue Tagore by Paul Muldoon, design by Faber, series design by Pentagram
The Happier Life by Douglas Dunn, design by Berthold Wolpe
Collected Poems by Wendy Cope, design by Faber
A State of Justice by Tom Paulin, design by Faber
Midsummer by Derek Walcott, design by Pentagram
Indiom by Daljit Nagra, design by Faber
To Aylsham Fair by George Barker, book cover by George W. Adamson, reproduced courtesy of the Adamson Estate
Essex Clay by Andrew Motion, design by Faber
Adam by Gboyega Odubanjo, design by Faber, series design by Pentagram
High Windows by Philip Larkin, design by Pentagram
The Poetry of W. B. Yeats by Louis MacNeice & W. B. Yeats, design by Berthold Wolpe

Every effort has been made to trace or contact all copyright holders. The publishers would be pleased to rectify at the earliest opportunity any omissions or errors brought to their notice.

NOTES

NOTES

NOTES

faber *academy*

Kickstart *your writing life* at Faber, the home *of British poetry*

From a one-day beginners' session to a six-month advanced programme, our range of poetry courses is designed to provide expert tuition and a supportive environment for poets at every level, both at our London and Newcastle venues and online.

For those not looking for a course, we also offer a range of manuscript assessments – get professional feedback on your writing from a published poet with a deep knowledge of the industry and a passion for the craft of poetry. Or join our mentoring programme and work one-to-one with a poet as you develop your work.

To find out more visit **faberacademy.com**

Become a Faber Member
and discover the best in the arts *and literature*

Sign up to the Faber Members programme and enjoy specially curated events, tailored discounts and exclusive previews of our forthcoming publications from the best novelists, poets, playwrights, thinkers, musicians and artists.

Join Faber Members for free at faber.co.uk

faber *members*